Sell Your House By Owner
And Save Thousands Of Dollars

Table of Contents

Money. The big reason most people decide to go For Sale By Owner (FSBO) or try to flip their house by their selves. But the decision of whether or not to go For Sale By Owner or FIY is a BIG decision. If you are reading this book you may be on the fence as to whether this is the right decision for you. Or, maybe you have already decided that this is the way to go and you just want to do it right.

Either way, in this book you will find helpful insights for both strategies and some fabulous resources to help you maximize your return on investment during the sale of your home. Whichever way that you decide to go, in the following chapters you will discover some great information that can help you every step of the way.

You will also discover some inside secrets to the behind the scenes workings of the real estate industry, and, you will learn from some of the top professionals in the field. Some of this information you probably already know. Some of it you can use to avoid the most common mistakes that FSBO's and FIY's make, and use this newfound knowledge to put more money back in your pocket.

If you are willing to learn the process, and invest the time and money to do it, you <u>can </u>sell your home yourself, <u>and save thousands of dollars in real estate agent's commissions</u>.

THIS BOOK WILL SHOW YOU HOW, STEP BY STEP!!

The techniques and suggestions in this book are not just some random ideas thrown together. They have been tested and proven over many years and thousands of successful sales.

This book is organized, and right to the point. Everything you need to know is here, but there's not a lot of fluff thrown in that would waste your time (You'll need every minute to work on the sale)!

Before we get started, I know that you may be thinking:

"Hey, wait a minute, why in the world would a real estate agent want to show me how to sell my home myself?

It does seem a little odd, but there is a perfectly logical explanation.

You see, when I first started my career in real estate, I joined the biggest, most popular real estate brokerage I could find. At this time I had already passed my real estate exam and gotten my license, so now that I found my chosen broker I just had to go through their 30-Day Training Program.

I went through the program and even managed to take my first listing and put it into escrow during my training!

Anyway, when I was going through training, one thing that I learned was that we only take 6% listings, that's 3% for us, the listing side, and 3% for the buyer's side.

I was a bright eyed and naive new agent and took that as law.

Well, one day, while visiting a For Sale By Owner, they admitted to me that they were ready to start talking seriously about listing their home with an agent.

We talked and got to know each other a little bit, and we really hit it off. I got the sense that they really liked me. We got down to the listing price, and I gave them my comparative market analysis (CMA), and then we discussed what my commission would be and what the cooperating agent commission should be.

I told them that I would need 3% for me, and 3% for the buyer's agent.

After some back and forth, they asked me if I would take 2.5%. I said no, I could not, and that I was firm at 3% for the listing side.

They said that they would need to think about it and get back to me.

The next day I learned that they had chosen another agent. I was heartbroken but I asked them what I could have done better. They said nothing, they really liked me, and they would have chosen me if I had just done the listing for 2.5%!

I was so upset! Not only were they a really nice family, but this was a $1,000,000 listing! The truth is I would have been happy listing it for 1% percent on my side!

Then I learned something that would change my perspective forever; we could take less than a 6% listing. Not only that, <u>many of the top selling agents in my office were listing homes for far less than 3%.</u> They would often list them at 1 or 1.5% in a half percent!

I couldn't believe it. How could they tell all of us new agents to list at 3% when they knew good and darn well the top agent we're taking considerably less. Well, as I discovered, these agents could become top producers because they could get more listings easier (because they were undercutting the heck out of the rest of us rookies) and take the listings for so little, because they would make it up by getting buyers from that listing and taking them to sell other people's listings where they could get full commissions.

Thus, my true my true real estate education began.

The Dark Side of the Real Estate Industry

Once I discovered the truth about the top performing agents, it changed my whole idea about the workings of the real estate industry. I continued to work hard and to target my most successful niches, For Sale By Owners and Expired Listings.

One reason that I had so much success in these areas was because of the high probability that these folks would be listing, and because I truly cared about getting their homes sold and their stories, and I believe that people could send my sincere sincerity.

I continued to make my calls every day, and stop by to visit FSBO's all around San Diego County. As I talked with many of the For Sale By Owners I discovered that many shared the same experiences, many had been hassled by agents, who all claimed to be "the best", and who all claimed to have buyers, only to find out that they just wanted to list the home.

I felt bad for these home owners, and wished that I could help. I knew that many of them did not have the equity to be able to list for 2.5 or 3%.

Unfortunately, I did not have the flexibility to be able to go lower at that time. I came up with some great ideas about how to be able to give home sellers the most marketing power and knowledge about selling their home without losing money.

Practically everyone I described my idea to thought it was great! But it wasn't until about 5 years later that I was able to take action on creating my ideal business model. A model created specifically with the For Sale By Owner, Do-it-Your-Self-er in mind.

But more about that later…

I mentioned before that I <u>am not</u> like most other agents you'll meet. I know that what goes around comes around.

In this book I will do everything I can to assist you so that you can achieve your goal of selling your home yourself, and there is absolutely <u>no obligation</u>.

<u>Here is the reason why:</u>

The facts are that nearly 90% of all the people that put their home up for sale by themselves eventually end up listing with an agent.

If your situation changes and you decide to list with an agent, I hope that you will allow me to show you my marketing plans and that you will at least consider me for the job.

If you are successful selling your home yourself (and your chances are excellent with the tips in this book), experience has proven to me that you may remember the help that I provided and give my name or pass this book on to others who might need my services.

In fact, I get more referrals from people who were successful selling on their own than the ones who end up listing. So I actually hope that you do achieve your goal and sell it!

No matter what happens, though, it's OK with me. I know that in the long run if I help enough people to get what they want, I will get what I want… which is to make a good living providing top-notch service to my clients.

So there you have it, pure and simple.

Now let's move on to the real task at hand… ***getting your home sold!!***

You <u>can</u> sell your home yourself, without listing it with a real estate agent.

Lots of work needs to be done, which means that you need to do the work of the agent. If you're willing to put in the effort and learn the process that top agents use, your chances of success will increase greatly.

First off, you need to adopt a business attitude about the entire situation. Homeowners are often quite emotional about their homes, and it can prevent them from making rational decisions when selling.

They reminisce about all of the holiday get-togethers, back yard barbecues, and how the family grew together in the home.

Potential buyers are not interested in nor affected by your emotional attachments to your home.

Potential buyers are not looking to buy your home, they are looking to buy a *house* that they can make into their home.

You must put your emotions aside and realize that you are going to have to make a dollars and cents business transaction.

Studies have shown that home sellers want three main things:

1) **To sell their home for the highest possible price,**

2) **within the time frame they need,**

3) **with the least amount of hassle and inconvenience.**

If you are like most sellers, you probably want the same things. Only since you are selling it yourself, you are willing to give up some on number three, because you are going to have to take on the work that a real estate agent would normally do.

Yes, that's right.

YOU MUST DO THE JOB OF THE REAL ESTATE AGENT!

Six-Step Home Selling Process

It can be a very overwhelming task, so the best way to tackle it is to learn and understand the six-step home selling process:

Step 1 - Understanding Market Conditions And Pricing Your Home

Step 2 - Calculating Your Bottom Line

Step 3 - Preparing Your Home For Sale

Step 4 - Marketing And Showing Your Home

Step 5 - Negotiation And Contract

Step 6 - Closing And Moving

Let's get right to it, and examine the six steps in closer detail!

Step 1 - Understanding Market Conditions And Pricing Your Home

This is by far the most important, yet most often misunderstood step.

Failure to understand the market and properly price your home is the single biggest factor that will cause it to NOT SELL for top dollar and sit unsold for months on end! Or, if you are like my neighbor a few doors down, not sell your house for 2.5 YEARS. Oh yeah, and he is a licensed real estate broker. Just goes to show you that there are lots of licensed agents and brokers out there that really don't have a clue what they are doing.

To make sure that this doesn't happen to you, you must first focus on two main areas:

1) CURRENT MARKET CONDITIONS

2) YOUR TIME REQUIREMENTS

Let's look at how current market conditions can effect selling and pricing.

Suppose that there were very few homes on the market for sale, and a large amount of eager buyers. What would that do to prices?

That's right, they would go up. This is referred to as a <u>seller's market.</u>

Conversely, if there were very few buyers and lots of eager sellers, what would that do to prices?

Sure, they would go down. That would be a <u>buyer's market.</u>

It is the basic laws of supply and demand.

Of course, that is a very simple example. Your local market may be at one of the extremes, or anywhere in between. You must consider things like interest rates, new home sales, and local economic factors such as large businesses opening or closing, etc.

To properly analyze your current market conditions, you will need to research homes *currently available, under contract,* and *recently sold* in your area.

There are several ways to get information on homes that have sold.

The first way is to do the research yourself. The sales prices of homes that have sold and closed is public record, so you can go to your county or city records office and dig for all of the information. I don't know exactly how long it would take, but don't make any other plans that day!

Many title companies will provide you with data on sold homes. Most will do this for free, to entice you to use them for your title insurance policy. For your convenience, I have listed my favorite title company in the resources section at the end of this book.

To get the most complete information, give me a call. With the click of a few buttons on my computer, I can have a complete computerized market analysis of your area (including available, under contract, and closed homes, average price per square foot, average days on market, etc.) printed out in a matter of minutes.

I will be happy to bring it over for you, *with absolutely no obligation, sales pitch, or pressure to list.*

Once you have the market information on homes in your area, take some time and drive around the area, stopping in front of the homes on your list. Make notes about the appearance and other details of the homes.

If any of the available homes are having an open house, take a look inside. Be up front with the owner or agent, and tell them, "We live in the area and are planning to sell our home ourselves. Do you mind if we take a quick look?"

This driving around is an important step, because it gets you more familiar with the market, and will help you make a more objective decision on pricing your home.

Next, sit down at the table and review the data and make honest, unbiased comparisons based on criteria such as:

SIZE
AGE
BEDROOMS
BATHS
POOL/SPA
BASEMENT
GARAGE
VIEW
LOT SIZE
OTHER FEATURES AND UPGRADES

Start by taking a brief look at the homes that are currently available for sale. The purpose of looking at the available homes is to get a feel for what other people in your area are asking, <u>NOT</u> to use the information to base your price on.

A seller can ask any price for their home, regardless of what it is really worth. Many of the available homes are priced in "dreamland". These prices DO NOT reflect the realities of the market. In fact, professional appraisers can not use available prices at all when appraising a house, only closed sales within the past six months.

Now move on to the pending and closed sales. This is the real bottom line, where the "rubber meets the road". It is the hard reality - what buyer's were willing to pay and what seller's were willing to sell for in a free, open market.

Study the closed sales. The first thing you may discover is that the actual sales price of the neighbor's home that sold 2 months ago is less than what they told you when you saw them out in the driveway. *Imagine that!*

Identify the homes that are similar to yours, ones that are nearly the same size, style, etc. Then look for items that are different like a remodeled kitchen, pool, finished basement, etc. and make adjustments.

DO NOT make the mistake of thinking that maintenance items can be considered as improvements that increase value. Things such as a new roof or new heating/cooling unit are really maintenance items.

While these items may make your home sell faster, they typically do not add much to the potential asking price of the home. After all, a buyer will expect a home to have a roof that doesn't leak and a properly functioning heating/cooling unit.

For example, let's say that there are 4 homes like yours that have recently sold, priced at $166,500, $169,900, $179,000, and $183,900. The home at $183,900 has some extra features that yours doesn't, but yours is superior to the one that sold for $166,500. Overall, the two other homes are pretty close to yours.

This gives you a current price range of $169,900 to $179,000. Now all you have to do is pick a price within this range!

Once you determine the proper price range for your home, how quickly you want to sell will dictate whether you price at the lower or higher ends of the price range.

This is where your own time requirements come into play.

Your own personal situation will have some effect on the price you ask for your home. It is easy to see that if you needed to sell your home within 4 days, you would have to price it lower than if you had 4 months to sell it.

If you were not in a major rush, but still wanted a sale in a reasonable amount of time, you might decide on an asking price of $175,000.

If you are still having difficulty determining the proper price for your home, you can call me for assistance (no obligation, of course), or hire a fee appraiser which you can find listed in the phone book.

It is natural for every homeowner to have a certain "pride of ownership" and to think that their home should be worth more than the one down the street. This is where you must be objective, and try to take your emotional attachments to your home out of the situation.

You must be reasonable. Unless you are in a total sellers market, if you price your home too high IT WILL NOT SELL!! It will sit on the market for months on end, getting the reputation of a "problem property".

People will assume that since the home has not sold, there must be something wrong with it. They will start to avoid it like the plague!

Even if you then drop the price, the damage is already done... the stigma is there, and you may need to drop the price even further to entice skeptical buyers.

DO NOT FALL INTO THIS TRAP!

Improper pricing is the single biggest mistake that sellers make. Don't let this happen to you. Make sure that you set a reasonable price for your home right from the start.

Step 2 - Calculating Your Bottom Line

Once you have determined a fair market price for your home, you can calculate your bottom line. This is the amount that you will net (get a check for) after paying all of the expenses associated with selling a home.

Remember, by selling your home yourself, the only cost you avoid is the real estate agent's commission. You will still have to pay all of the other closing costs, just like any other seller.

Closing costs vary from area to area and also depend on how each individual contract is structured. The following are items that you may need to deduct from your sales price to determine your net proceeds:

> **MORTGAGES OR LOANS** - Any first, second, etc. loans, or mortgages. Also any liens that occurred if you used your home as collateral. Call or write your lender and ask for the amount to pay the loan in full (often not the same as the principal balance).

> **LOAN DISCOUNT POINTS** – In many areas it is customary for the seller to pay points on the buyers loan. This is negotiable, except on certain government loans. One point is equal to one percent of the loan amount (not sales price). For example, if the sales price was $175,000, and the buyer put a 10% down payment of $17,500, the loan amount would be $157,500. One discount point would be $1,575, two points $3,150, etc.

> **PRORATED INTEREST** – Mortgage interest is generally charged in arrears. This means that when you make your July payment, you are actually paying interest for June. So if your home sale closes on July 26th, you will still owe interest for 26 days even though you already made your payment on July 1st.

> **BUYERS CLOSING COSTS** – Many buyers will ask the seller to pay part or all of their closing costs. On some government loans it is required by law that the seller pay them. These costs can include, but are not limited to: loan application fees, credit report, loan

origination fee (usually 1% of the loan amount), loan discount points, title, escrow, and attorney's fees, funding fees, tax service, mortgage insurance premiums, and impounds for taxes, insurance, and interest.

- ➤ **ATTORNEY FEES** – Everyone loves lawyers!

- ➤ **ESCROW FEES** – Escrow companies are disinterested third parties that hold funds, handle paperwork, and make sure that all necessary conditions are **met** before releasing money or transferring title.

- ➤ **TRANSFER TAXES/CHARGES** – Transfer fees are often charged by state or local governments as a way to increase revenue. They vary widely, and are often based on a percentage of the sales price.

- ➤ **APPRAISAL FEES** – If the buyer is obtaining new financing for the purchase, the lender will require a professional appraisal on the house. This is another negotiable item, but is often paid by the seller in some areas.

- ➤ **TERMITE INSPECTIONS** – Required on some government loans, and requested by many buyers.

- ➤ **STRUCTURAL/GENERAL INSPECTIONS** – Professional independent inspection services are required by law in some areas and often requested by buyers to make them more confident about the purchase. I have a great inspector recommendation in the resources section at the end of this book for your convenience.

- **TITLE INSURANCE FEES** – Title insurance protects the buyer and lender against issues of improper ownership or transfer. The title insurance company will research the title to make sure there are no liens, judgements, or clouds on the title that would effect the ownership rights.

- **HOMEOWNER ASSOCIATION FEES** – If the area has an HOA, chances are that there will be a fee to transfer from one owner to the next.

- **PREPAYMENT PENALTIES** – Many private and some conventional loans have specific monetary penalties if the loan is paid off prior to a certain date.

- **RECONVEYANCE FEES** – This fee may be charged by an attorney or escrow company to clear off the lien on the title when your existing loan is paid off at closing.

- **FAILURE TO NOTIFY PENALTIES** – Some government lenders can charge one extra months interest if you fail to notify them at least 30 days in advance of your intent to pay off the loan.

- **ASSUMPTION FEES** – Loans that are being assumed by the buyer often have an assumption fee charged by the lender.

➢ **HOME WARRANTY COVERAGE** –Depending on the plan, a home warranty covers items in the house (plumbing, electrical, appliances, etc.) for a period of usually one year.

For a list of specific charges, you can contact a title/escrow office, mortgage lender, or a real estate attorney. Of course, I would be happy to provide you with a net proceeds analysis at _no cost or obligation_.

After completing the first two steps in the process, it is entirely possible that you may decide not to sell after all. Perhaps the market values are not what you had thought, and you won't be able to net enough money on the sale to be able to accomplish your next goal.

The important thing is to accept the realities of the market. If the timing isn't right for you, it isn't right!

Step 3 - Preparing Your Home For Sale

Properly preparing your home for sale can make the difference between a quick sale at full price, and a home that sits unsold for months… even after several price reductions.

The first order of business is to forget your emotional attachment to your home and look at it through the eyes of a potential buyer. Be impartial, and recognize the weaknesses of your home.

How does it stack up?

Remember, potential buyers are going to be viewing lots of other homes, and if yours doesn't stand out, it will be much more difficult to sell.

Buyers buy what they see. **If what they see is dirty, messy, and worn looking, you don't stand a chance.**

It's just like if you were going to sell your car. The first thing you would do is clean and "detail" the car inside and out. Your house is no different!!

With a mental picture of a model home in your mind, make an "attack list" of items to be completed on your home. It may be a short or long list, depending on the condition of your home, but keep in mind that all your efforts now will pay off big on closing day.

The objective is to make your home appear well maintained, spacious, organized and clean. Many factors such as how light it is, the colors, sounds and smell subtly effect the buyers impression of your home.

Start by walking out to the middle of the street and take a good, focused look at the overall appearance of the exterior of your home. Good "curb appeal" will make the critical proper first impression. Remember, if a home is unattractive from the outside, buyers won't bother to see the inside!

This means well groomed, healthy looking lawn, trees, shrubs, and flower beds.

Check your driveway and clean any oil stains with cleaning solutions, and move any old vehicles, trailers, or boats off the premises to a storage facility.

Replace or repair any loose or missing roof shingles or tiles.

If needed, replace or repaint the mailbox.

Your front door is a focal point of potential buyers. Make sure it is scrubbed clean or completely refinished if necessary.

Fix any broken windows or screens.

Completely repainting the exterior of your home may be necessary if it is peeling or blistering, but often simply doing the trim, window sashes, shutters, and garage door is sufficient.

Remove any political or other signs.

Now do the same to the side and rear yards. Remove all debris, junk, and clutter. Clean and neatly arrange any lawn furniture, barbecues, etc.

Next move to the inside of your home.

Begin with a complete, top to bottom, military-style scrubbing of every room, nook and cranny. Be especially diligent in the kitchen and bathrooms, which should pass the white glove test. <u>Clean houses sell</u>!

Attack the garage and basement, if you have them. Now is the time to get rid of any old junk, and clean and organize everything else.

If the interior hasn't been painted in several years, you should probably go ahead and do it. A fresh coat of white or off-white paint will make the place look bigger and lighter, and give it a "new" smell. It doesn't cost that much, and makes a big difference in buyer perception. If not, do a thorough job of touch-up painting.

Have the carpet cleaned. If it is worn, replace it. This is a fairly big cost, but it makes a huge difference in how the home shows. You should more than make up for the expense with a faster sale at a higher price.

Install the highest intensity bulbs allowable in all the light fixtures. This will make the rooms appear larger, brighter, and more cheerful.

Clean all windows and curtains/blinds.

Clean out the closets to make them look bigger. Store out of season clothes elsewhere and neatly arrange what's left.

Too much clutter will make a home feel small and disorganized. Move out excess furniture, especially worn or outdated items, and take down pictures that hide the walls. Clean off the magnets from the refrigerator, and box up any other clutter-causing nick knacks.

Clean all the heating/cooling system vents, and replace the filters.

Fix or replace all of the little things that you have been meaning to get to. Make sure that <u>everything</u> is working properly (toilets, appliances, doorbell, etc.)

If you have lived in your home for a while, by the time you finish with your attack list you will probably have truckloads of stuff to either sell, give away to charity, or take to the dump. Your motto should be: **"If in doubt, move it out"!!**

Consider having a huge garage sale. Not only will you reduce the clutter in your home, but you can use the proceeds to pay for some of your touch-ups and repairs. Plus, movers charge by the pound, so you'll save there too!

Make sure that your cars are clean as well. It all adds to the impression that you are people that take good care of your things.

If you smoke, DO NOT SMOKE IN THE HOUSE!! A smoky smelling house turns buyers off faster than nuclear waste, *even buyers who smoke themselves*!

If you have smoked in the house much, you will probably need to paint the interior, and have the carpets, drapes, and furniture deep cleaned.

This brings us to pets. While household pets may be nice for everyday living, they are one of your worst enemies when it's time to sell.

If you have pets, you'll have pet odors, whether you notice them or not. About 25% of prospective buyers will not consider a home with pets in it - either because they have allergies, or simply think it is dirty. Plus, a dog barking, sniffing, and scratching hardly makes a potential buyer feel relaxed and comfortable.

If at all possible, see if a neighbor, friend, or relative will take the animal until the home is sold. I know you may be quite attached to your pet and this may be a touchy subject, but it's up to you if you want a sale for top dollar.

It can be a lot of work, but it will be worth it. Clean, organized, clutter-free homes are always the first to sell!

<u>Step 4 - Marketing And Showing Your Home</u>

Now that your home is ready, it's time to find some interested buyers to show it to. The effort required to attract potential purchasers depends on the current market conditions in your area.

If you are in the midst of a sellers market where there is a shortage of homes for sale, simply throwing a FOR SALE sign out in the yard can produce a frenzy of activity.

Unfortunately, most markets are nowhere near that good, so you better plan on putting in some long hours. You are competing with all of the other homes for sale, and the competition is often fierce.

The first step in your marketing plan is to put up a for sale sign in the front yard. Before you run down to the corner drug store, keep in mind that a cheap, flimsy looking sign does not convey the quality image that you want. Invest some money in a nice looking, quality sign that will last longer than the first rain storm.

It should be at least as nice as the ones that the real estate agents use. Call some sign painters and get some bids.

Next, put together a professional looking brochure that communicates all of the features and benefits of your home. Include a nice picture of your home and touch on such items as proximity to schools, shopping, major transportation routes, major employers, and recreation areas.

Also cover neighborhood amenities, age, appearance, condition, bedrooms, bathrooms, type and style, landscaping, garage, kitchen, family room, laundry, pool/spa, basement, etc.

Don't forget financial information such as the price, down payment, monthly payment, year round utility expenses, property taxes, what items are included in **the** sale (such as appliances, shelving, etc.), and of course, directions to the house along with your name, address, and phone number.

A representative from a local mortgage company should be willing to provide you with all of the information you'll need regarding loan programs, down payments, interest rates, monthly payments, etc.

With personal computers, desktop publishing is much easier than ever before. If you have access to a computer, you should be able to put together a nice looking brochure if you take your time and think it through. Please… *no junky looking flyers!*

If you can't do it yourself, sketch out a rough draft by hand and take it along with a picture of your home to a quick print shop. They should be able to fix you up fairly inexpensively.

Once you have your brochures, you need to have a weatherproof information box to put them in next to (or attached to) the yard sign. The box should read: FREE

INFO - PLEASE TAKE ONE. Monitor the box and keep it full.

Also pass out the brochures to all of your friends and neighbors, pass them out at area businesses, drop some off at the relocation office of any large employers in the area, and put them up on bulletin boards wherever possible.

Now write a good, enthusiastic sounding ad to run in the newspaper. Try to make your ad stand out from the others. It is important to have an attention-getting HEADLINE such as:

"MOVING TO TEXAS"   "OUR LOSS, YOUR GAIN"
"DIVORCE FORCES SALE"   "YOU WON'T BELIEVE THIS"
"MUST SELL QUICK"   "SPACIOUS HOME NEEDS LOVING FAMILY"
"WALK TO SCHOOL"   "ENJOY PRIVACY"

Test different ads and see what the responses are. You can try running a different ad each week, or a different one in separate publications.

Focus on the benefits of your home. Don't write a boring ad that sounds like all the others and will get lost in the crowd. Stress items such as views, quiet street, landscaping, master bedroom, kitchen, and family room.

The whole purpose of the ad is to get your phone to ring.

THIS MEANS THAT SOMEONE NEEDS TO ANSWER IT!!

The biggest complaint that buyers have with for sale by owners is that no one answers the phone when they call… or they get a child or babysitter that is not prepared to handle the call properly.

You are competing against professionals. You need to be home, or utilize a cellular phone, call forwarding, or pager. If a buyer can't get through to you, they often just go on to the next ad or call a real estate agent.

Keep a copy of your brochure next to the phone, it can help you stay organized and not miss any features when callers inquire. If callers don't want **to set an** appointment yet, offer to mail them a brochure.

Also keep a call log handy, so you will know how many calls you are getting from which ads, and to keep track of names and phone numbers.

Look into all possible avenues to market your home. Your area may have a FOR SALE BY OWNER magazine, or cable TV program, etc.

Sites like Craigslist, ForSaleByOwner.com and House Trader are also great resources.

Many of these ideas cost money, so you will have to pay some things out of pocket to be able to get your home this type of exposure. Of course, if you are able to sell it without a listing agent then you should save significantly since you won't be paying a listing commission.

An Open House can help get your home exposed to the market. Get some directional Open House signs and place them at corners leading to your home from major streets, and one in front of your house. Make sure to check local regulations before placing signs. You also may want to run an advertisement in the newspaper, Craigslist, the Union Tribune, and now Realtor.com if you are in the MLS. Many newspapers and online sites have separate Open House sections.

Be sure to put up plenty of signs so that people can easily find your open house, and have lots of flyers ready to go.

Snacks and drinks, especially bottled waters are a nice thing to add to the experience that potential buyers will have when they walk into the house for the first time.

I am now going to suggest an option that can add a large amount of exposure to your home and still save you half of the normal commission you would pay an agent.

Before you have a heart attack, I am not talking about listing it with an agent. You do not have to use this option, but in most markets it makes a lot of sense.

On your sign and in all of your ads, insert the words "Agents Welcome". When agents call, tell them that you are NOT listing with an agent, but that you will be happy to pay them a 2.5-3% commission if they bring you a buyer that successfully buys your home.

This commission is about the same as an agent would make if they sold another agents listing, and a majority of homes are sold by an agent other than the listing agent.

This option can generate a lot of additional interest in your home. If an agent does end up selling it, not only will you still save a substantial amount compared to a full commission, but you will have professional assistance along the way, as well.

As they say, pictures are worth a thousand words, so be sure that you get some really nice shots of your property. Use a wide angle lens in small rooms to be able to show the whole thing.

If you know how to create a virtual tour, this is definitely worth doing. If not, you can go to the resource guide at the end of this book and discover how to get a professional virtual tour and webpage done for relatively inexpensive. In your ads, whether it be Craigslist or House Trader, it's important to post as many (good) pictures as possible. This will entice buyers to come see your home.

- o   Here is a checklist of items to include in your ads:
- o   # of beds/baths
- o   square footage
- o   flooring, carpet/tile/wood
- o   countertops
- o   school district
- o   upgrades
- o   view
- o   pool/spa
- o   amenities

o freeway access?
   etc.

This will give you a good start. Be forewarned, even if you put "no agents" in your ad, expect many agent calls. It's just the nature of the business.

Once you have attracted interested buyers, it's time to show your home. This is where all your time and effort in preparing your home will really pay off!

Before you set an appointment, make sure that the buyer is looking for what you have. If they need six bedrooms and you only have three, they probably won't be serious about your home.

Also take a few minutes to politely "qualify" the buyer by asking questions about how long they have been on the job, do they own a home currently, have they been pre-approved for a loan by a lender, etc.

You don't want to waste time showing your home to prospects who can't afford to buy it! Or worse, spend weeks in escrow with a buyer that can't get the job done!

Also, a few words of caution. People are not always who they seem, and you can never be too careful. One look at the newspaper or evening news is proof enough.

It is recommended that you ask for identification and the license number of their car prior to letting strangers into your home. Serious buyers won't mind, especially when you cheerfully tell them that it is simply a security precaution that was recommended to you.

Stash all small valuables out of sight. Even though you will try to stay with the buyers as they tour your home, you never can watch them completely.

It is probably a wise idea for women to avoid showing the home without someone else present. This is not intended to be sexist, just cautious. You decide for yourself.

OK, it's ShowTime!

To get the most out of every showing, there are certain procedures you should follow, both prior to the buyers arrival and after they come in.

Shortly before the appointment, open all of the drapes and blinds and turn on all the lights, … even in the daytime. Turn off the TV and put some soft music on low volume. Set the thermostats so that it is not too hot or cold. If you have children, send them to a friends, or put them on their best behavior.

If you still have pets in the house, get them out and freshen the air. Make sure all of the beds are made and do a quick pick-up throughout.

When the buyers arrive, your home should sell itself. Be friendly and cheerful, and try to make them feel comfortable. Hand them your brochure, and take them on a tour of the property.

Show the most appealing parts of your home first. Casually point out all of the features and benefits of your home, but don't oversell or say stupid things like "this is the kitchen".

If they are not interested, they will probably politely thank you and head for the door. Don't take it personally, the layout or something else about the house probably just doesn't fit their personal needs.

If the buyers are interested, you will know it. They will stay longer, and ask lots of questions.

If they show serious interest, don't be afraid to suggest that they buy it!

Once you have a serious buyer, you first must figure out if they are truly qualified. If you are working with a buyer agent, they should have already qualified the buyer, however, unfortunately, they don't always do a very good job.

And, even if they do a good job, with the lending laws always changing, a good buyer can become a not-so-good buyer very quickly. This is when it pays to have a lender on your side. A good lender will cross qualify for you.

Now be warned, some buyers agents may not appreciate this, but it is fair in the current state has things to have a second opinion on the qualifications of your potential buyer.

A good lender will be interested in doing this for you if there may be a chance that they will get business from it. If your buyer does not have an agent, then this lender can and should be willing to put their money where their mouth is. By this I mean, if they are not able to close on time, they should be willing to pay you for every day over the closing date that they go.

Granted, most lenders are not willing to do this, even though most lenders will tell you that they've been in business for any number of years and have closed so many transactions and are such an expert and blah, blah, blah.

The reality is that many still have trouble getting the job done, and some of it is not their fault. In fact, many times they are battling with underwriting, and trying to get through red tape, so this is just a warning. But this can make or break your transaction so push for a pro. You can find my top picks in the resource section of this book.

It's time to get a signed contract!

Step 5 - Negotiation And Contract

Being familiar with the market conditions and knowing your personal motivation to sell will guide you in the negotiations.

Get a standard real estate purchase contract and make sure that you are completely familiar with it and how to fill it out. Review it with a real estate attorney if you are not comfortable.

Generally, the buyer will present you with an offer for you to consider. In most states, only written contracts for the purchase of real estate are enforceable, so make sure it is in writing, not merely verbal.

The buyer may not have the proper forms, so always make sure to have several contracts ready to go.

Starting negotiations face to face with the buyer with both of you staring at a blank page can be a bit awkward, but just keep your objectives in mind and forge ahead. Politely but firmly take control of the situation.

This is where things can get a little sticky, and you will need to have done your homework. Having a contract that is not worded properly can put you into a real hornet's nest.

If you have multiple offers, it can get even trickier because you may be negotiating on different terms with each different offer.

This is also the most dangerous time if you are not skilled or experienced in negotiating your real estate transaction. Unfortunately, it is easy to make a mistake, and worse, if there is a buyer's agent involved, a good buyer's agent has a legal to teach to negotiate to the best of their ability for their client. In some cases this is to your great disadvantage.

Most agents are fair and honest so in most cases you have nothing to worry about. However, there are many who are either inexperienced, or straight-up untrustworthy. Worse yet, some are even downright unscrupulous.

This is one of the most dangerous aspects of selling your home yourself. If you end up not protecting yourself properly it could cost you.

Make sure to spell out every little detail in the contract. A misunderstanding (honest or otherwise), could end up costing you thousands of dollars or even tying your home up for months.

When you are presented with an offer from a buyer, you have three basic options:

1) Accept the offer

2) Reject the offer

3) Make a counter offer

Here is some items that you should consider when structuring an offer or deciding how to respond to an offer that is presented to you.

- ✓ PRICE
- ✓ DOWN PAYMENT
- ✓ EARNEST MONEY DEPOSIT (MINIMUM 2% OF SALES PRICE)
- ✓ IS THE BUYER PRE-APPROVED
- ✓ IS THE INTEREST RATE THEY WANT AVAILABLE
- ✓ CLOSING/POSSESSION DATES
- ✓ PRORATIONS
- ✓ LOAN DISCOUNT POINTS - WHO PAYS
- ✓ CLOSING COSTS - WHO PAYS WHAT
- ✓ APPRAISAL - WHO PAYS
- ✓ HOME PROTECTION PLAN - WHO PAYS
- ✓ INSPECTIONS - WHAT TYPE AND WHO PAYS
- ✓ ITEMS INCLUDED (WASHER/DRYER, REFRIGERATOR, ETC.)
- ✓ TITLE/ESCROW COMPANY/ATTORNEY
- ✓ CONTINGENCIES - WHAT AND HOW LONG

Contingencies may seem like a minor issue, but they can be a major stumbling block. A contingency means that something else must happen in order for the deal to go through.

A purchase may be contingent on the buyer getting approved for financing, selling the home that they already own, getting a favorable inspection report, or any number of other things.

Make the contingencies as specific as possible, and spell out exactly what will happen if the contingency is or isn't met. Also, try to make them self-canceling. For example: *"If buyer does not object in writing within 14 days from acceptance of this offer, contingency shall be considered removed".*

At this point I would also like to mention that you must disclose anything and everything that you have done to the property, or that a previous owner has done, or anything that you know that would be considered a material fact.

A "material fact" in real estate law basically means that if the buyer had known about it, they may have changed their mind, or changed their offer.

Besides messing up negotiations, the second biggest mistake that FSBO's make is not disclosing properly. When in doubt, disclose! This step is extra important because it can come back to bite you years after your transaction has closed.

There are plenty of contracts that you can use to help this process, for example, local area disclosures, national hazard disclosures, and there might be others depending on your location.

As you probably already know, we live in sue happy times, so it is extra important to get these disclosures done, and done right. Speaking of disclosures, here is a disclosure of my own: this is not legal advice. Use this information at your own risk. If you would like more specific advice please feel free to contact my office toll-free at 1-800-859-9010 ext. 0 for the front desk.

There are companies that specialize in producing reports that will help you to make sure that you are disclosing all of the natural hazards. I have listed my favorite companies in the resource is section of this book.

Spending some extra time to make sure that the contract is "clean" can save you enormous headaches down the road!

Once you have a contract mutually agreed upon and signed by all parties, take it with the buyers earnest deposit to an escrow company or real estate attorney

Closing And Moving

You are on the home stretch, almost there!! Now is not the time to get lazy or drop the ball.

Once all of the terms and conditions of the contract are agreed upon by you and the buyer, you will really need to stay on top of things on a daily basis. There are at least a hundred things that can go wrong and foul up the sale.

You will probably be dealing with a mortgage company, title company, escrow company or attorney, appraiser, and inspector, among others. Make certain that the buyers deposit check clears the bank, that their credit report and other financial information is O.K., and that all deadlines and contingencies are met.

Make darn sure that everything is in order BEFORE you start loading things into the moving truck. You don't want to have to put the house back on the market after you have moved out! Plus, once you move out, the buyer has a lot more leverage to get you to alter the contract in their favor.

Don't forget the little details like transferring the utilities out of your name, and change of address for U.S. mail and newspapers.

Specialized Resources – The Evolved Home Seller Proprietary Method

Technology has in many ways leveled the field for home sellers to compete with professional sales agents.

That isn't saying that there isn't value in having real estate experience, negotiating skills, marketing skills, market knowledge, etc. There is tremendous value with these skills.

But, the good news is that there are many new models out there that can facilitate smoother transactions for less cost than traditional brick and mortar big box brokers.

Most sellers these days still prefer to go list with a big box broker, pay full commissions, and take a beating on their return. I can't blame them, that is their choice. They like the familiar, the names they have heard of and trust, and don't mind spending extra for it.

There are also home sellers, For Sale By Owner types, that understand the internet, understand their local market, and have some confidence with the tools available to them, and most importantly, aren't afraid to jump in and get their hands dirty.

For this second group of folks, I developed some tools and systems that can give them the added edge to add money to their pockets, without paying heft commissions.

Because, let's face it, in the market today home buyers and sellers or are more technologically savvy than ever before. Not only that, access to information is more readily available than ever before too. This combination should allow buyers and sellers to connect more easily, and theoretically, cut out the middle man, or the middle men, as it were.

This is easier said than done of course as a For Sale By Owner, this is what you are banking on. So here is the deal, as I said before, I believe that you can do it. Most agents would hate me to tell you this, believe what is the best time in the history of Real Estate to go for it yourself.

However, I would be remiss to not tell you about some of the challenges and dangers that you will face. So, in order to help make the process as smooth and profitable as possible for you, I have created a business model that I think you will agree provides you with the most powerful marketing tools, the most flexible fee structure, and the best resources available.

Plus, you get access to professional experience, at a fraction of the price. Thus, putting more money in your pocket. So here's how it works...

First, when you have come to the decision to cooperate with an agent, the next logical step is to get your listing in front of as many agents and buyers as possible, so you're gonna definitely want to put your home in the MLS.

Because I work with a "virtual broker," or "net broker," that means my broker does not have expensive overhead like a physical office, or huge advertising costs, so I pay an extremely low flat fee per transaction.

I pass this huge savings directly to you so that I can offer a low flat fee to put your home in the MLS. At this point, I will not help you market your home in any way, or negotiate, so you are on your own, but you will have plenty of buyers and buyer's agents contacting you as long as you price your home reasonably.

However, if you want to really maximize your exposure then I would recommend that you purchase some of the marketing packages that incorporate professional ad copy, templates and tools that you can then customize to fit your needs.

The most popular option gets you on the MLS, gets you a professional yard sign complete with your own 24 Hour Recorded Message featuring a Virtual Tour of your house that buyers can call any hour of the day or night, plus a custom QR Scan code so they can instantly see a Virtual tour of your house while they drive by.

The calls will be forwarded to you for your convenience and follow up, and you get the same tools that I used to become a Top Producing real estate agent for a fraction of the cost. You can get all the details by calling the **free recorded message, toll-free 24/7 at 1-800-469-0902 ext. 1879 or go to <u>www.EvolvedHomes.com/fsbokit</u>**

Next, you will probably get some offers. Here is where the negotiations take place, the best and most dangerous part of the sale, and should not be taken lightly. If you are experienced, then have at it. But if not, I would strongly urge you to take advantage of my hourly negotiation and contract review rates.

Yes, you will pay more than if you just go for it yourself. But for the peace of mind, and for the risk avoidance, I personally and professionally think it is well worth the investment. Nothing hurts worse than a bad case of the "would-a-shoulda's". Because if you do make a bad deal you may lose days off the market or worse, thousands, or even tens of thousands of dollars.

You will probably also want some help with contracts and again, this is money well spent in my opinion. However if you choose to go it yourself, you can, then there is never any pressure. Why? Because I have a life. Yeah, I actually do other things than real estate. I am a musician. I have a family. I have multiple streams of income. I don't say this to brag, just to explain why I have created this tool that allows you to save the money someone in my position would normally charge.

This business model allows me to work with my favorite kinds of folks, the DIY's (that's Do-It-Yourselfer's) who do most of the work themselves, and therefore deserve to keep most of the money themselves. I know, it sounds like real-estate-agent-suicide to tell you that I don't live, breathe and die real estate. But the reality is, this is to your benefit. No pressure from me. You have the power, I am here to support you if you want it.

Finally, you will close escrow and get your money! Of course, it is not all as easy and quick as it sounds, there is work involved. But, for you to have the option of how much work you want to do is priceless. This is where my model is especially attractive to most For Sale By Owners and Do-It-Yourselfer's. It's not for everyone, but if this makes sense to you, please take a look at the details located at www.evolvedhomes.com/sellfsbo

Flip Your House And Get Someone

Else To Foot The Bill!

This sounds almost too good to be true, right? You want to sell your house. It needs work, you don't have the funds or want to spend the money to do the upgrades but you know that you would make considerably more money selling if you had these upgrades done.

What are your options?

First, you could go to the bank, try to get a loan, if you get a loan, find two to three reputable construction or remodeling companies, haggle for the best price you can get, pay them, hope they get done in a reasonable amount of time, put your home on the market and hope to sell for more than you put into it.

This could work, but it's not guaranteed and you're liable to the bank if you can't pull it off.

If you do go this route however, be very cautious about where you put your money into upgrades. I know that you want to save money, but doing a cheap job or worse yet, doing an expensive job but in a style that is not massively appealing can cost you money up front and on the sale.

If you are doing upgrades consult a designer or do your homework and find out exactly what the homes that are selling look like, what brands, styles and colors they use.

You want to go conservative here.

According to Realtor.com, "Kitchen and bathroom updates can be costly, but the return on your investment ranges between 75 to 100 percent."

The Realtor.com site goes on to state the top 10 improvements are:

- Kitchen
- Bathroom
- Home exterior ("curb appeal")
- Home siding
- Roofs
- Decks
- Flooring (especially hardwood floors)
- Room addition
- Window replacements
- Master bedroom

But chances are, if you haven't done the upgrades while you have been living there, you shouldn't try to speculate on the market and put money in now. You won't get to enjoy it and if you can't get the job done for a low enough cost, or your house doesn't sell for the amount you need, or you can't find a buyer, you will be stuck with more payments.

So this route, while possible, isn't a great way to go.

But you know that you are missing out on a huge opportunity not doing these upgrades so what to do?

What if you could find someone that would pay for the construction costs, do the work, and then split the profits with you without any money out of pocket from you?

Well there are a few such people who are willing and able to do this sort of transaction.

NOTE: This is not investment advice, and this is not legal advice. Get proper counsel and advice from qualified professionals in your area!

These types of investors may or may not be investing in your area. To find someone you could put ads in the local newspaper, on Craigslist.com, or maybe start calling construction companies and pitching the idea to them and explain the type of deal you are looking to work out.

Explain the terms, consideration, collateral, split, timelines, etc.

Really do your homework and check them out before doing business. Check their references and past deals. Ask the folks what their experience was like.

If you are in the southern California area you may qualify to work with some of my investors.

After a simple, free application process you could qualify to have the remodel of your home done by professionals that have been in the business for years and you wouldn't have to spend a dime to do it out of pocket to do it.

This allows you to maximize your potential profit from the sale of your home. Don't let thousands of dollars slip through your hands, see if you qualify.

Simply fill out the free application at www.EvolvedHomes.com/fiy. Or, **call the toll-free 24**

hour free recorded message at 1-800-469-0902 ext. 8876.

Working with someone who has done this kind of transaction before can be very useful. They know what things to fix up to get the most return, they know what color schemes and styles are selling right now. An accomplished company can be a great asset to your home selling for the most profit.

And, they put their money where their mouth is. They are fronting thousands or tens of thousands of dollars in materials and labor to make these improvements. This is far and away the best way to go about flipping your home if you can.

Don't delay, find out today if this is an option for you.

IN CONCLUSION

I hope you have found this book to be a valuable source of information to aid you in selling your home yourself. If you follow the tips and recommendations outlined here, you will be way ahead of most others attempting to sell their homes or flip their homes themselves.

If you are considering doing any kind of serious upgrades, seriously consider finding a company that specializes in doing flips so that way you can get the most money out of the sale of your home.

Combining this Do-It-Yourself flip strategy with the EvolvedHomes.com tiered service packages you can remodel your house with no money out of pocket, sell for more money because of the new upgrades, net more on the sale because you are leveraging the Evolved Home Seller Method™ to save thousands on real estate commissions.

You are one smart cookie!

Good luck and save money!

"Million Dollar Rolodex" Resources

Here is a list of the "Diamond in the Rough" Real Estate Vendors and Service Providers that I have found to be the best in the business. This resource guide alone will save you time, money and energy! Be sure to tell them that you found them through this FIY/FSBO Book! (And Winston!)

Escrow – Legends Escrow
        Joe Salvatore… 858-449-5412
        jsalvatore@legendsescrow.com

Joe is the coolest guy you will ever speak with and his team is very knowledgeable and experienced. During your negotiations be sure to specify Legends Escrow for escrow in your Residential Purchase Agreement, you can thank me later. (Be sure to tell him "Winston sent me!"

Title- Corinthian Title
        Kachina Krafchow....619-925-2523
        Kachina.Krafchow@corinthiantitle.com
        www.CorinthianTitle.com

Home Inspections – Nowak Inspections
        Damion Nowak… 619-857-8461
        NowakInspections@gmail.com

Lender- (Get Your Buyer's PreQualified!)
        Franklin Advantage
        Mike Perez..........949-246-0633 (Office)
        949-246-0633 (Mobile)
        mike@mikelending.com
                (be sure to tell 'em Winston sent you!)

Home Warranty- CRES/HISCO Home Warranty
Dave Miller… 858-945-3974
Dmiller@creshomewarranty.com

Carpet Cleaning- Xfactor Carpet Care
Ron Keil - 858-245-7698
Email : o.ronald@att.net

Carpet, Hardwood, Tile, Sales/Installation-
Customer Service – 800-469-0902 x 8867

Cash Buyer – Get Cash For Your Home in as little as 10 days
1-800-469-0902 ext. 1880
cash@evolvedhomes.com
www.evolvedhomes.com/cashbuyer

Garage Doors - Coastal Garage Doors
Mike … 619-507-0140
www.GarageRepairsSanDiego.com

Staging- Consider It Staged
Yvonne Marquez…619-884-1406
Yvonnestylist@cox.net
www.Consideritstaged.com

House Cleaning- Your Conscious Cleaners
Rachel Lizzet … 619-788-1958
YourConsciousCleaners@gmail.com
www.YourConsciousCleaners.com

Handyman/Handyperson – Chix Who Fix
   Nikki and Darla – 619-715-2828
   (tell 'em Winston sent ya!)

Printing (for flyers) – Copy-It
    619-698-7000
    info@copy-it.com
    www.Copy-It.com

MLS and Marketing – (800) 469-0902 ext 0
    info@evolvedhomes.com
    www.EvolvedHomes.com/sellfsbo

Professional Virtual Tours (800) 469-0902 ext 0
    info@evolvedhomes.com
    www.EvolvedHomes.com/tours